# Shopify

*Create Your Very Own Profitable Online Business Empire!*

JONATHAN S. WALKER

Copyright © 20127 Jonathan S. Walker

All rights reserved.

# DEDICATION

I dedicate this book to my two beautiful children and my loving wife who have been nothing short of being my light and joy throughout the years.

Copyright 2017 by Jonathan S. Walker - All rights reserved.

The following eBook is reproduced below with the goal of providing information that is as accurate and reliable as possible. Regardless, purchasing this eBook can be seen as consent to the fact that both the publisher and the author of this book are in no way experts on the topics discussed within and that any recommendations or suggestions that are made herein are for entertainment purposes only. Professionals should be consulted as needed prior to undertaking any of the action endorsed herein.

This declaration is deemed fair and valid by both the American Bar Association and the Committee of Publishers Association and is legally binding throughout the United States.

Furthermore, the transmission, duplication or reproduction of any of the following work including specific information will be considered an illegal act irrespective of if it is done electronically or in print. This extends to creating a secondary or tertiary copy of the work or a recorded copy and is only allowed with express written consent from the Publisher. All additional right reserved.

The information in the following pages is broadly considered to be a truthful and accurate account of facts and as such any inattention, use or misuse of the information in question by the reader will render any resulting actions solely under their purview. There are no scenarios in which the publisher or the original author of this work can be in any fashion deemed liable for any hardship or damages that may befall them after undertaking information described herein.

Additionally, the information in the following pages is intended only for informational purposes and should thus be thought of as universal. As befitting its nature, it is presented without assurance regarding its prolonged validity or interim quality. Trademarks that are mentioned are done without written consent and can in no way be considered an endorsement from the trademark holder.

# VIP Subscriber List

Dear Reader, If you would like to receive latest tips and tricks on internet marketing, exclusive strategies, upcoming books & promotions, and more, do subscribe to my mailing list in the link below! I will be giving away a free book that you can download right away as well after you subscribe to show my appreciation!

Here's the link: http://bit.do/jonathanswalker

# TABLE OF CONTENTS

## Part 1

Introduction

Chapter 1: Establishing Your Own At-Home Product for Sale

Chapter 2: What Shopify is and How to Use It

Chapter 3: The Basics of Dropshipping

Chapter 4: How to Maximize Your Profits with Amazon FBA

Conclusion

## Part 2

Introduction

Chapter 1: What Dropshipping Entails

Chapter 2: Tips on How to Create a Successful Dropshipping Business

Chapter 3: How to Make Shopify Work for Your Business

Chapter 4: Tips on Dropshipping with Shopify

Chapter 5: Amazon FBA User Secrets

Conclusion

**Part 3**

Chapter 1: How To Gain More Reviews

Chapter 2: Strategies To Sell Products on Amazon

Chapter 3: Strategies for Getting Product From Suppliers

Chapter 4: Understanding The Ranking System on Amazon

Chapter 5: Products – The Good, The Bad, and The Ugly

Part 4

Chapter 1 – Create An Ebook Empire

Chapter 2 – Create Killer Blogs

Chapter 3- Create Your Own Youtube Channel

Chapter 4 – Sell With Amazon FBA

Chapter 5 – Create Membership Sites

# Introduction

Congratulations on purchasing your personal copy of *Shopify: Create Your Very Own Profitable Online Business Empire! (Make Money from Home, Shopify, Dropshipping, Amazon FBA)*. Thank you for doing so.

This book is going to provide you with all of the information that you need to know regarding three types of tools you can learn to use in order to make more money from home. These three methods include Shopify, dropshipping, and Amazon FBA. After learning about each of the methods that are presented in this book, you will have all of the information that you need to start working towards your goal of becoming an online entrepreneur. These tactics are not complex; however, many people end up using these potential revenue streams incorrectly. This book will help you to navigate these various tools properly. That's why this book is important.

The final chapter in this book will discuss how to use Amazon FBA as a way to make money. After reading this book, you'll be one step ahead of the game in the sense that you're going to be less likely to make mistakes, and more likely to capitalize on what's possible in your pocket and bottom line.

Again, thank you for purchasing this book, *Shopify: Create Your Very Own Profitable Online Business Empire! (Make Money from Home, Shopify, Dropshipping, Amazon FBA)*. Enjoy the rest of what it has to offer!

# Chapter 1: Establishing Your Own At-Home Product for Sale

Before you begin using any of the online forums that are going to be discussed, it's important that you first establish the type of product that you're going to sell. If you already have a product that you're selling online, then you've completed this step, but you may also be in a situation where you don't know what you're interested in selling at all. Let's take a look at some considerations you need to be making so that you can use Shopify, dropshipping, and Amazon FBA to the fullest extent possible.

**You Need a Product**

It's important to understand that in order to use the three online revenue techniques that are going to be discussed later, you need a physical product to sell. Selling a service, or selling something that is made digitally will not allow you to use the three platforms that are going to be discussed in this book. This does not mean that you need to create this product from scratch yourself. Instead, you can opt to re-sell a product that you get for a discount and then can charge your customer full price. You can also adapt a product that is already on the market. Below are a few considerations to make while you're figuring out what it is you'd be interested in selling for profit:

**Keyword Research**

SEO stands for Search Engine Optimization, and SEO research has become one of the primary ways that aspiring online entrepreneurs figure out what is in high demand on the internet. Keyword research involves understanding what people are typing into their Google search bar the most often and then cater your website to fits needs that already exist. If you're interested in doing some keyword research of your own, some of the best SEO websites include the following:

- Google Keyword Planner
- SEMrush
- SpyFU
- Serpstat

Unfortunately, keyword research is a marketing tool that is currently in high demand. For this reason, a good keyword search tool is not going to be free. In fact, these tools can cost you upwards of $20 per month; however, if you're serious about getting an online business going, it's worth it. Keep in mind, when you're doing keyword research, you want to find keywords that are high in search volume but low in competition. Most of these SEO tools will provide you with a percentage of how competitive the keywords that you're searching are.

**Notice a Trend as Early as Possible**

You don't want to be targeting a niche that already has a lot of competition within it. For example, if you wanted to sell yoga mats online, you are going to be competing against major corporations like Lululemon. Your product is likely to drown against competition that has millions of dollars behind it. If you can, you should begin to think about and notice trends that could be up and coming. Then, target those as soon as you can. Social media and other internet avenues can help you to figure out what these trends are.

# Chapter 2: What Shopify Is and How to Use It

Once you've figured out what it is you're going to sell, you can then work towards figuring out how you're going to set up your online presence and brand. A great way to accomplish these types of goals is through a service known as Shopify. Shopify can be best described as a platform that makes creating an online store as easy as possible. Let's go through the steps that you'll need to take in order to set up an online shop through Shopify.

**Step 1: Sign Up**

The first thing to do when you're looking to open an online shop with Shopify is to sign up on their website. Simply head to www.shopify.com, provide them with your email address and click on the large blue button that says, "Get started." Remember, you're going to want to provide Shopify with the email address you want to use for your online shop, rather than your personal email address. From here, Shopify will also ask you the name of your business.

**Step 2: How Will You Use Shopify?**

After you've provided Shopify with your basic information, it will then ask you whether you plan on using Shopify as an online store, or as a tool that you will be using inside of a physical store where you rent or buy space. Finally, it will also ask you questions that have to do with the types of taxes your store will be paying. These questions include ones related to where in the country your store is located or where you will be conducting your business from when you're online. They will also ask you whether you're already selling product and what your annual revenue is expected to be.

**Step 3: Add Your Products**

Next, add your products to your store's page. You will need to upload pictures of what you're selling, along with descriptions of the item, and the item's cost.

**Step 4: Make Your Store Your Own**

Once you've uploaded the products to your online store, the last step involves heading to Shopify's dashboard. From here, click on the tab that's labeled, "Customize the Look of Your Site." This tab allows you to change features of the store's layout itself and will also allow you to truly make your online store your own. Changing these features does not require programming knowledge, which will make customizing your site a breeze.

**Shopify's Domain Platform**

Shopify allows you to either add a domain name from scratch or transfer a domain that you already own to your online Shopify profile. Within your dashboard, click on the tab that's labeled "Add a Domain." From here, you will be provided with the option to register a new one or add one that's already been purchased. If you are purchasing a new one from Shopify, this will cost you around $9.00 for the year. As you can see, Shopify makes it easy to both purchase a new domain or transfer one.

**How to Get Paid**

Finally, the last aspect of Shopify that is crucial to turn on is the payment processor. Again, head to the dashboard and click on Payments. From here, you can choose from many different payment processors. Shopify also has its own payment processor. Once you've chosen the type of processor you'd like to use, be sure to click on "Launch Website." Please keep in mind that if you're transferring a domain, you may need to wait a few days before the domain that you're transferring has been linked to your online Shopify store.

# Chapter 3: The Basics of Dropshipping

If you're not interested in setting up your own online store and are instead looking for a less formal way to make money via the internet, then dropshipping may be just the route you want to take. This chapter will discuss the ins and outs of dropshipping so that you can maximize your revenue with this particular method.

**The Logistics of an Online Business**

One aspect of the online store that Shopify does not account for is shipping. If you're serious about developing an online method of profit for yourself, then the way in which you're going to ship your products to your customers is an important consideration that you need to be making. When you're thinking about this, there are a few factors that you need to take into account. These include how to keep your shipping costs as low as possible, and where you are going to store your product inventory. If the product that you're selling is small, then storage will likely not be an issue for you; however, if you're planning to sell products that are bulkier, then storage space is something that you'll likely need to have. This where dropshipping can come in handy.

**Shipping to Your Customer from a Vendor's Website**

If you're not planning to actually create a product yourself to sell, then you can instead simply advertise goods on a website and then ship them directly to your customers from the vendor's website. To do this, all you would have to do is create a price for the product on your website that will allow you to still make a profit after accounting for shipping costs. You will also probably need to spend money on advertising your products, to ensure that people will buy them. It's important to note that you're likely going to get more bang for your buck this way if you choose to promote products that are on the expensive side. This way, your profit margin will likely be greater than if you choose to sell products that are cheaper.

**How to Negotiate with a Dropshipping Service**

While purchasing a product and choosing to ship it directly to a customer can be perfect for someone who is simply going to be re-selling a product, if you are creating something that you've made to sell online, then you may not be able to simply ship a product from a vendor's site. Instead, you will have to negotiate with a dropshipping service. This will require some legwork. First, you'll have to reach out to find a drop shipper who will be willing to discuss doing business with you. You'll also have to figure out whether or not this company would be willing to store your products for you in their warehouse. Lastly, you may want to find out whether or not this distributor would be willing to put your logo or company's name on their packing slip when they ship your product for you. This will make your product seem more professional, even though it is being shipped from an auxiliary source.

These days, there are plenty of websites that have

already worked through the process of negotiating with a dropshipping service on your behalf. Some of these websites include WholeSale Central, Alibaba, and Oberlo. For all of these sites, you can find products that fit the theme of your website and can be drop shipped from a manufacturer. Not only will using these types of websites save you time; they will also allow you to cut down on the cost of resources such as tape or boxes. These shipping costs can add up, which is why dropshipping can be a lucrative tool to use when you're looking to operate a simple, yet effective, online business.

# Chapter 4: How to Maximize Your Profits with Amazon FBA

The FBA in Amazon FBA is short for Fulfillment by Amazon. If you've ever wondered how Amazon can reach such a large audience of people and seems to have any type of product you can ever imagine, the answer in part has to do with Amazon's FBA program. This service essentially allows you, the seller, to host your products on Amazon's website. This means that if you decide that your website is going to sell running shoes, then you can post the products that you're selling to Amazon's website. If someone sees your running shoe product and wants to purchase it, they are able to do so through the Amazon platform. This allows you to reach a wider range of people than would otherwise be possible if you were simply selling on your own smaller Shopify website. Let's take a look at how Amazon FBA works in more detail.

**How to Become Involved with Amazon FBA**

Becoming a seller through Amazon has never been easier.

After you've opened up a seller account through Amazon, you will then be prompted to start uploading your products to your seller portal. Once your products have been placed on Amazon's website, you will then need to ship your products to an Amazon shipping center. You can print out a shipping label from your Amazon FBA portal. This shipping center will essentially be the place where your products will be stored until someone buys them. Once purchased, Amazon will handle the process of shipping your product to its customer. It's also important to understand that you are still able to sell the products that you send to Amazon from other online platforms. If you end up selling your product to a customer on Etsy for example, Amazon will honor this sale and ship the product back to you. This provides you with the added flexibility of being able to sell your products on multiple platforms simultaneously.

**The Cost of Amazon FBA**

Amazon FBA is not free. In fact, it will cost you a little over forty dollars per month if you want to start using this service. In addition to forty dollars, Amazon will also charge a fulfillment fee for each product that you sell. This means that they are taking a cut of whatever you're selling for themselves. For example, if you were to sell a $50 pair of running shoes through Amazon and charge a $10 shipping fee, you are going to end up with $51 after the sale has been completed. This means that if you originally bought the shoes for $50, you're only going to be making a $1 profit. This is why it's important to understand your profit margins for each product prior to selling them on Amazon. Lastly, it's also important to keep in mind that Amazon is going to discount your shipping rates to them once you subscribe to Amazon FBA. Additionally, many items that are sold through the Amazon FBA program and offered to customers with a free shipping option. This feature will undoubtedly entice your customers to purchase.

# PART 2

# Chapter 1: What Dropshipping Entails

While you can certainly develop an e-commerce website without dropshipping, it's more than likely that you will be spending more money than you need to if you don't use dropshipping. This chapter is going to discuss exactly what dropshipping is, so that you have a firm grasp on how dropshipping is defined and what it's all about. We will also get into some of the finer points of dropshipping, so that you can have an edge on your competition when it comes to delivering products to your customers efficiently and without error.

**The Dropshipping Supply Chain**

It's important for you to understand how a dropshipping supply chain works in its entirety, especially when you're interested in starting a business based around this concept. **Dropshipping Supply Chain Component 1: The Manufacturer**

The manufacturer can be best described as the

product's point of origin.  When the manufacturer agrees to sell their product, they will normally do so only when the retailer or seller agrees to buy a certain quantity of the manufacturer's product.  For someone like you who is probably going to be expensing this e-commerce business yourself, purchasing product in bulk from a manufacturer may not be realistic.

## Dropshipping Supply Chain Component 2: The Wholesaler

If you do end up purchasing product from a manufacturer, you would be considered a wholesaler. These are the people who buy the product from the manufacturer in bulk quantities, increase the price of the good so that they can make a small profit from it, and then sell it to retailers.  Generally speaking, a wholesaler is not going to sell their product to an individual.  They are still looking to sell the manufactured product to a retail store.

## Dropshipping Supply Chain Component 3: The Retailer

The last aspect of the dropshipping supply chain consists of the retailer. The retailer is the supply chain component who ends up selling the product to an individual consumer. They too are going to increase the price of the good so that a profit can be made. As you can see, the price of the product has been increased at least twice before it makes its way into your life when you decide to purchase something at a store. From an entrepreneurial perspective, this is why dropshipping can matter. If you can insert your business into the dropshipping supply chain, you have the potential to make money off of the profit margins that can be seen between the wholesaler and the retailer.

# Chapter 2: Tips on How to Create a Successful Dropshipping Business

As should be obvious after reading the previous chapter, there is money to be made in the business of dropshipping, especially when you consider the reach of the internet. These days, people do not exclusively purchase the products that they want from big retail stores such as Target or Walmart. Yes, these types of companies are hugely profitable, but people are now known to shop on much smaller internet websites. For this reason, using dropshipping as the primary backbone for an e-commerce business could be the perfect way for you to make money from home. This chapter will provide you with some essential tips on how to do exactly that.

**A Definition of Dropshipping**

As the name suggests, dropshipping can be best defined as a method of shipping that eliminates the middle-man. In other words, when you own an e-commerce drop-shipping business, you're never going to have the product in your physical inventory. Instead, you simply process the order for your customer and then have the dropshipping service ship the product that your customer purchased directly to them. This saves you time, money, and resources.

**Tip 1 to Starting a Dropshipping E-Commerce Business: Find Your Niche and Stick with It**

Once you create an e-commerce website, your business will have an identity of some type. This identity is going to dictate the type of products that you sell. The types of people whom you're going to attract to your selling portal will likely depend on the types of products that you're selling. For this reason, it doesn't make sense for you to sell many different types of products. For example, being in the business of selling yoga mats and fishing gear both on the same website is silly from the perspective of brand identity. This is where the notion of a niche website comes into play. A niche site is one that is only looking to attract a very specific type of audience. To obtain a good niche site, keyword research is needed. After finding a keyword that yields good results from a competition perspective, you can then begin to think about what types of products you're going to sell on your e-commerce website.

## Tip 2 to Start a Dropshipping E-Commerce Business: Communicate with Your Customers

We have all probably dealt with items being incorrectly shipped to us while in transit. Products can arrive at a customer damaged, or a package can get lost in the shuffle of making its way to the customer. For these reasons, it's important that you communicate with your customers about how your business operates. When their order is placed, inform them that it will be coming from a dropshipping service. It would also be a good idea to provide your customer with their tracking number as soon as you're informed that their product has been shipped. This is a form of preventative maintenance that will put your customer at ease before any problems even arise.

## Tip 3 to Start a Dropshipping E-Commerce Business: Don't Fall for a Fee

If a dropshipping service is trying to tack on a bunch of fees, you should take your business elsewhere. Take the time to find a dropshipping company that does not charge you a shipping fee. After all, you're trying to run a business. Even if the fee that a particular company charge are low, it's still going to add up to expenses that will have to come out of your company's pocket.

# Chapter 3: How to Make Shopify Work for Your Business

In conjunction with dropshipping, Shopify is another great online tool that can take your e-commerce business to the next level.

**The Cost of Using Shopify**

As with many other types of online services, you have a few options regarding how much you'd like to pay Shopify when you're using their amenities. They do allow you to try their online store with no credit card required for fourteen days. This is something that not all online services allow. After the two-week trial period, you then have the option of paying either $29 per month, $79 per month, or $229 per month. It's also important to note that there are no fees that you need to pay Shopify when you are using their online portal, as long as you're conducting your business over the internet.

In other words, if you have a brick-and-mortar store, you're going to have to pay a transaction fee to use your Shopify portal in your store. The less that you pay Shopify on a monthly basis, the higher your transaction fee is going to be when you're using Shopify in a physical store. For example, when you pay Shopify $29 per month, Shopify is going to take 2.0% of all of your transaction profits for the month. If you're paying Shopify $79 per month, they are only going to take 1.0% of your profits for the month.

**The Perks of Each Shopify Account Type**

As you can see, Shopify seems to be rewarding its users who do not have physical stores. If you do own space in a physical store and are considering using the Shopify service, you want to make sure that you're still going to make a significant profit after you pay Shopify. If you don't figure out this type of math before purchasing Shopify, you may end up finding that Shopify is not worth the cost in your particular situation.

Other features that will vary depending on the type of account that you choose to purchase include the number of staff members who can access your portal, the shipping discount that you'll receive from Shopify, and the ability to provide your customers with the option to buy gift cards. On the other hand, all Shopify store types allow you to upload as many products as you'd like and will be able to offer you unlimited file storage. You'll also be able to integrate any other blogs or websites that you already have into your Shopify account, as well as be provided with 24-hour customer Shopify support.

As you can see, it is possible to make money on Shopify, as long as you know what you're doing. It's important to figure out what you anticipate your income is going to be before signing up for Shopify and then choosing your Shopify package type based on these calculations. This way, there be less guesswork involved and you will have an accurate idea of how much your dropshipping business will be able to make while using Shopify's services.

# Chapter 4: Tips on Dropshipping with Shopify

So far, we have talked about both dropshipping and Shopify. Now, it's time to combine the two. This chapter is going to provide you with tips on how you should design your Shopify portal if you're going to be dropshipping.

**The Layout of Your Shopify E-Commerce Platform Matters**

After you've figured out what you're going to be selling, your next step is to create your Shopify site. Below is a list of the pages that you should consider for creating your Shopify profile when you're going to be dropshipping:

1. **Contact Page:** Your business is going to suffer if your customers do not feel as if they can easily get in touch with you. This page should include at least your

company's email address, and perhaps a customer service phone number as well.

2. **Returns Page:** Figuring out how you're going to handle returns is an extremely important part of any dropshipping e-commerce business. Mistakes happen, and customers are going to sometimes inevitably be unhappy with their purchase. Where should these customers send their products, and what will your return policy entail?

3. **Shipping Page:** Outlining your shipping process on a page of your website will likely allow your customers to feel like they're "in the loop." Setting up a shipping page that outlines what your customers can expect when they're dealing with your company will likely decrease the number of questions your customers may want to ask you.

4. **Product Page:** Your product page is going to be the bread and butter of your e-commerce business. You want your product page to look sharp, professional, and clean.

5. **About You Page:** Similar to your shipping page, the *About You* page will likely comfort your customers, especially if they're initially weary about dealing with you. Remember, trust can be an issue on the internet at times. You want your customers to feel safe on your website, and your about me page can serve as a welcomed "Hello!" to anyone with whom you are not directly interacting,

6. **Homepage:** As with any website, the homepage on your Shopify profile should be easy to navigate and access. It should identify how you can get to the rest of the

pages on the site, and also look as professional as possible.

# Chapter 5: Amazon FBA User Secrets

This last chapter is going to look at how you can optimize your online business strategies through the use of Amazon FBA. Fulfillment by Amazon is a way that you can expand the reach of what you're selling by gaining access to Amazon's elite and extensive website. Let's take a look at some top tips from people who have been dropshipping through Amazon FBA for years.

**FBA Secret 1: Treat it Like a Business**

While Amazon FBA is not the same as having your traditional website up and running where you sell products to people, you should still treat the time that you spend on Amazon FBA the same that you would like an e-commerce business. Even though using Amazon FBA allows you to move away from creating your website, this does not mean that you should not take Amazon FBA seriously. You can lose money through this platform if you're not accurate in your estimates or you're sloppy with your profit margin calculations.

**FBA Secret 2: Peruse Amazon**

Another tip that many Amazon FBA users miss is that they don't do research on the Amazon site itself before deciding which products they're going to sell. Even if you enjoy fishing, this does not necessarily mean that selling fishing poles on Amazon is a decision that is going to lead to profits. Look at what's selling the most frequently on Amazon, and take note of any markets that may look like they're being underrepresented.

**FBA Secret 3: Diversify Your Product Line**

Unlike the notion of a niche website that we've already discussed, you do not have to worry about keeping a product line that is similar when you're using Amazon FBA. Because your seller profile is not going to define the type of business that you're running, you have the freedom to pick and choose the products that you want to sell. This can be great for someone who is good at doing research on products within Amazon's website. By figuring out the profit margin that's possible from certain products that are on the market, you should be able to make better financial decisions for yourself and your business.

# PART 3

# Chapter One: How to Gain More Reviews

Reviews are vital to your business on Amazon if you are wanting to sell more product. The more reviews and the better your reviews are, your chances will increase on others buying your product. While it is sometimes hard to believe, more and more people are looking at the reviews on the products that they are wanting to buy off of Amazon so that they can decide if your product is going to be the best one for them to buy or if they should continue looking for someone else who may have the same product but at a lower price.

Customers of Amazon have guidelines that they are required to follow whenever they are leaving a review on the site about a product. Therefore, if you are trying to get reviews from people that you know or by offering discounted or free product to customers on Facebook or through an email promotion, you need to make sure that your customers know what the guidelines are for leaving a review on Amazon so that you are not losing reviews due to someone not putting a review up that met Amazon standards.

Amazon review guidelines:
- You can ask customers that have bought your product before to leave a review by sending them a newsletter or posting something on social media. This is one of the best ways to get an honest review because you already have a customer that has bought your product and apparently likes you because they have subscribed to your newsletter or liked your page on social media.
- Make sure that you are offering excellent customer service. Most bad reviews come from poor customer service due to the fact that they feel as if they are being misled by the

product's description or they contact you over an issue, and you do not respond, or you are rude when you do respond.

- After someone has made a purchase, send out a follow-up email to ask them to leave a review of the product that they purchased from you.
- Amazon ranks its top reviewers, and you can solicit the top reviewers by offering them your product in exchange for an honest review. If you are looking for someone that is on the top reviewer's list, you are going to see a title next to their name such as "Top Ten Reviewer" or "Hall of Fame Reviewer."
- Another way to get reviews is to go to the pages that offer a product that is similar to yours and find their reviewers. You may not get the customer to buy your product, but you can learn what you should and should not do

with your product so that you can get better reviews than your competitor.

Those are just some of the ways that you can get reviews. There are other ways that you can get reviews but ensure that you are following the rules that Amazon has put into place, or you are going to end up getting reviews taken off of your product due to the fact that the rules that Amazon has put into place for the reviews, no matter what method it is that you are using.

# Chapter Two: Strategies to Sell Products on Amazon

Not only are reviews important, but the way that you market your product is important as well. If you do not give the proper description for your product, or you do not provide quality pictures of your product, then you will not find a lot of customers who are going to be willing to purchase your product.

The best method to selling your products is to use Amazon FBA. When trying to sell on Amazon, it is vital to have a strategy on how you are going to sell your product. There is no promise that you are going to sell enough of your product in order to make up for all the money that you will spend in manufacturing it. But, that is the hope correct? Hopefully, through the use of some well-placed strategies, you can not only make up for production costs but also make a profit too.

As you have probably already figured out, the rankings on Amazon work like this. The more sales you get plus, the more reviews your product receives, the higher your ranking is will be on Amazon. But, we are going to go into further detail in that in chapter four so that you can fully understand the ranking system as it applies to Amazon.

The strategies that we are about to discuss are meant to not only help you sell more product but help you to get more reviews so that your Amazon ranking goes up! There are a ton of different tactics that you can use besides the ones that are discussed in this chapter.

- Amazon Ads: if you are selling on Amazon, you need to be using Amazon Ads. Through the use of Amazon ads, your keyword rankings are going to increase because your product is getting more exposure. Amazon ads are only available for sellers on Amazon.

Ads can be accessed through the "Campaign Manager" through the Amazon Seller Central.

It is a good idea to start off with automatic targeting so that your promotion ads reach as many people as possible. Keep in mind, the higher that your daily budget is, the more exposure your ad is going to get. After there have been a couple of hundred dollars in your sales, then you will be able to run your report so you can determine which keywords are being searched the most for people to find your product. From there you are going to set up your manual targeting and use those specific keywords that people are searching in order to find your product online.

- Give away some of your product: this does not mean that you will just be giving away product for free. Instead, you are giving away product for a lower price than what you are attempting to sell it for. Sell it for a dollar or two so that more people become interested in it and buy it.

By offering your product for the cheaper pricing, you are going to sell more products and most likely gain some more reviews which is going to assist you in raising within the rankings of Amazon.

A good way to be sure that millions of people are not just buying your product for a dollar or two is to hand out coupon codes to your friends and family as well as their friends. This will allow them to purchase your product for the lower price and then once they have purchased your product, you will have the ability to confront them and see if they are willing to leave an honest review.

In doing this, you will more than likely break even or risk losing money instead of making money. The primary thing that is going to determine how much money you earn or lose is going to determine how much it costs for you to manufacture your product. So, in order to make sure that you do not lose too much money, you are going to want, to begin with a product that is not expensive to produce.

- Tomoson is a website that will grant you access to the world of thousands of bloggers that are just standing in line to receive your product for a review as well as promotion.

Tomoson allows you to set up a free trial so that you can see how well it works for you. You are going to need to list your product there and then respond to the emails that you are going to get from the bloggers that are excited to help promote your product.

Through this, you are going to be required to give your product to the bloggers for free. But, you can always provide them with a coupon that is going to allow them to get it for a dollar so that you are still getting money and not violating any of Amazon's review rules.

After they have received the item that you have supplied them with to review you are going to want to ensure that they do the following so that you are able to get more eyes on your product.

- o Leave an honest review on Amazon
- o Post the product and their review to their social media pages
- o Post a review on their blog with a link to the Amazon page
- o Create a YouTube video that will link it to Amazon

You will realize that many people are going to be perfectly fine doing all of this for you just to test the product that you are selling. But, there are a few blogs that you will come across that will end up having a fee in place to promote your product. This fee can be as little as five dollars and go as high as fifty.

It is a good idea just to pay the fee if the blog is big enough and will enable a lot of sales from that blog.

- Buview and Zonblast are just another way for you to sell more product and rise through the Amazon ranks.

These resources are going to be aimed towards Amazon sells in order to help with the promotion and sale of your product on other people's lists. This can end up meaning that you have to "give away" products but, even if you just use coupon codes, there is a likelihood that you are going to get a decent return.

A major drawback is that you are going to have to pay money to use services such as Buview and Zonblast, but if you do not have it in your budget to do so, you are not required to use these services. It just another strategy that you can use in order to improve your sales.

Keep in mind that you are going to need to reserve a significant amount of your stock before you purchase these services or else your inventory is going to quickly be wiped out. You will need to closely monitor your inventory so that you know exactly how many items you are giving away or selling through the use of these services.

- Last but not least there is always Facebook; you can use Facebook ads as well as fan pages that will help you pull customers and sell products.

# Chapter Three: Strategies for Getting Product from Suppliers

Having a relationship with your vendors is important because they are going to be your partners. Suppliers are going to be the people that help support you when you are trying to get the goods that you need for your products.

The suppliers are going to be the people that will advise you with information as well as assist in evaluating any new items that you may potentially be wanting to sell. Suppliers also contribute in identifying design flaws and offering ideas on how you can improve these weaknesses so that you are able to cut costs and sell more product than your competition.

It is easy to try and go with the first supplier that

offers you a good deal; however, you are not going to want to do that. You are going to want your supplier to help you grow rather than stay stagnant. Having a good relationship with your supplier leads to improved service that you receive from that vendor's company. By improved service I mean that the supplier is going to tell you what does not work for you and your company, you will receive discounts on the supplies that you need, and ultimately it leads to a better buyer/ supplier relationship.

In order to create a good relationship with your vendor you will want to:

- Know the lingo by learning the basics of the industry. That way you can show your vendor that you are open to learning but that you are going to advocate for yourself on the deals that you get with your vendor.
- Do not compromise on communication.

- Look up what the actual costs are so that you can better negotiate a price.
- Think like the supplier. They want to sell you something, and you want to buy it so that you can sell it. Therefore, you will want to show that you are a resource to that vendor's company instead of a risk.

# Chapter Four: Understanding the Ranking System on Amazon

Your product's ranking on amazon is going to determine how many potential customers see that product when they are browsing the Amazon website. The higher the ranking for your product is, the more people are going to see it. So, what you are going to want to do is raise your Amazon ranking so that your product is seen over your competition's product.

- Your ranking is going to be dependent on the search bar. How often does a customer search for your particular product? The search bar is one of the biggest factors in your ranking because this is where all of the customers look for the products they want to see.
- Keep your product title under sixty characters.
- Use the bullet points Amazon offers so that your customer can see what they need to see

about the product such as dimensions of the product.

- Be descriptive about your product! Your product description is what sells your product.
- Do not skip over the keywords. These keywords are going to assist in customers locating your product so that they can buy it rather than buying your competition's product.

Your ranking on Amazon can also go up if you use an ASIN, the ASIN is going to make it to where you can compete in prices, but you are going to be placing your product on someone else's post as a way to try and redirect the customer so that they come to your product page rather than the one that they are currently on. This means that you have to offer your product for a lower price, even if that price is a penny less than what the competition is offering theirs for.

# Chapter Five: Products – The Good, The Bad, and The Ugly

Having a good product to sell on Amazon is going to make it to where you can make a profit off of Amazon. However, there are also going to be products that you are not going to want to sell on Amazon. It is vitally important that you know the difference between the products that you want to see and the products that you are going to want to be away from.

When you look through Amazon, you see that just

about everything can be sold on Amazon. While this is great, that does not mean that you need to sell whatever on Amazon, you are going to want to stick to the products that are going to push you through the ranking system while making you a profit and having customers coming back for more.

- The product you offer should be light so that you are saving yourself the headache of a product being damaged when it is shipped. This will also save on shipping costs and even customs costs if it is being shipped overseas.
- Ensure that your product is easy to manufacture so that you are leaving less room for error in the production of the product. You want your product to be high quality.
- Try and keep your product under two hundred dollars. There is going to be a greater risk to you if you are selling a product that is going to cost more than two hundred dollars because

you are taking on a greater risk and that product will most likely require a higher level of quality control.

- Stay away from the products that you would buy. If it is something that everyone buys, go the other way with your product so that you do not have to compete with the big box stores where a customer is going to be able to go to get the product right away rather than wait for it to be shipped.

- Seasonal stuff is great to sell, but you are going to end up not having any sales the rest of the year. If you are going to do something seasonal, then make sure you have other products to sell as well it also helps keep excessive inventory down.

- Some products have to have warranties on them if they break down, try and steer clear of these products so that you are not losing money in replacing parts that may have broken in shipping. This will also make sure that you are not opening yourself up to a lawsuit.

- Lastly, trademarks are going to end up getting you sued in the event that you do not obtain the proper permission needed to sell it. But, keep in mind, if you buy it from overseas, it is most likely not an authentic product.

With this list, you are going to have a decent place to start when it comes to selling product on Amazon and what you should stay away from.

# PART 4

## INTRODUCTION

Haven't you heard every successful internet entrepreneur worth his courses and blogs talk obsessively about passive income? Their focus is always on creating solid, multiple and life-long streams of wealth. So, what exactly is passive income? Why is it such a buzzword among online marketers? Why is everyone scurrying to harness the power of the internet to create income streams that last forever?

We've all been a part of the daily grind that trades time for money. We trade specific numbers of hours and get paid for only those many hours. And there's a perpetual financial crunch when it comes to meeting our expenses. To fill the gap, we take on part-time jobs, work overtime, work weekends and unfortunately, it is still not enough. We are still trading time for money. There are but 24 hours in a day, and there's only so much we can make if our income is equivalent to the time and effort we put in a day. How then does one experience exponential growth in income without spending a fortune? How does one always have enough money to enjoy the good things life without slogging night and day? Passive income is the key.

Notice how some people have all the time in the world but no money to enjoy the time at hand, while others have all the money they need but no time to enjoy the money since they are busy using that time to make money. Passive income gives you both. The time to enjoy the money you earn and the money to enjoy the time at hand. Unfortunately, a majority of the folks are so caught up in the concept of financial security that they sacrifice their financial freedom for it. True financial freedom comes when you have both time and money to enjoy your life without thinking about where the money for your next bill will come from.

As life progresses, you realize that you've traded financial freedom for financial security, where your time, income and efforts are controlled by someone else. You realize that you've been a bucket carrier all your life who goes to work on a particular day, works according to the dictates of others and then brings home a bucket of water (income). Contrast this with passive income, which is more like building a pipeline of wealth. When you create a pipeline of capital, the water automatically flows from the tap whenever you want it to. You don't have to go out and put in hours of hard work and time to get the water home in a bucket. When you create powerful, practical and multiple sources of income – the income simply comes gushing to your house. It isn't a natural process of course, but nothing in life that's worth having is ever easy. It may take days or months to create a pipeline, but it is a one-time effort that can give you a lifelong source of income. To quote an oft repeated internet marketing cliché which is indeed true, with the passive income you literally make money while you are sleeping. Or holidaying in the Alps. Or attending your child's school function. You do not have to work large numbers of hours to rake in a substantial income.

Now there are many ways to earn passive income. You may think of owning real estate and leasing it out as a form of passive income. Then some investments can give you a sound passive income based on the interests these investments generate. However, think about the upfront investments these sources of income require. Purchasing pricey real estate or setting aside a huge sum for investment purposes is no mean feat. You may make a decent amount of passive income in return, but the investment may just not make it worth it.

Let us look at online passive income streams now. They require minimal investment and can help you witness exponential financial growth. Other than a low investment, all you need is time and information to get started, and you may well be on your way to creating a treasure house of income. Most well-known online entrepreneurs didn't start as millionaires. They barely had enough money to pay their bills and sustain. They were just perceptive, tenacious and resourceful enough to channelize the power of the internet to create smart income streams. There's no reason why you cannot do the same.

This book has just about everything you need to know about building passive income streams online. I have tried my best to share the little-known strategies and proven secret sauce that differentiates average internet marketers from the really successful ones. There are lots of actionable points and nuggets of wisdom that can help you build strong, diverse sources of passive income online with little investment. You will learn how to think out of the box and become an innovative online entrepreneur. More than anything - you will discover the joy and gratification of creating sources of wealth that give you greater freedom. Think -the freedom to spend time with your loved ones, the freedom to live life on your terms and the freedom to work for your profits rather than the net profits of a corporation. Get on the passive income lane now and enjoy the ride!

# Chapter 1: Create an eBook Empire

Well yes, the truth is - people are loving eBooks. A comprehensive 2012 survey by Pew Research Center discovered that about 43 percent of Americans read a book or long content (journals, magazines, etc.) on an electronic device. The survey also revealed about 28 percent Americans owned a minimum of one electronic reading device. You can only imagine how much the numbers would have grown since. Packed with practicality (well, even the biggest home library may not be able to accommodate a million books), portability and quick access, eBooks are transforming the way people read. Why not cash in on this wonderful development and create some useful, information-packed and exciting books that will add value to people's lives? Here's all the meat and juice for creating your own successful eBook empire.

**Find a Passion**

We all have that one thing which lights the fire in us. What is that one topic or niche which you can talk on or write about for hours? Fitness? Psychic powers? Cooking? Raising children? Write down a list of possible ideas you can think of which you see yourself writing with knowledge and passion. Build mind maps once you've decided on the core topic. These can include all the sub-topics you may want to include within the main subject. For instance, if you are putting together a fitness related eBook, think of all the chapters/sub-topics/sub niches to be included in it.

This can be fitness workouts, diets to complement your workouts, ideal fitness attire, fitness gear, fitness stretches and the likes. Similarly, if you find the marketplace is already crowded with too many fitness related books, you can narrow down your focus to a single aspect of fitness. Say Post Pregnancy Fitness – How to Get Back in Shape After Having a Baby. If you are already an expert in a particular niche, such as a child psychologist or real estate attorney or wedding planner, jump right in within your area of expertise.

## Start Writing

Once you have a topic in place, begin a rough table of contents draft for the book. This will help you flesh out the topics later. You can use any word processor such as Notepad or Word. Some people prefer Evernote. If you are not comfortable writing it as a single document, break down the documents chapter-wise. This way you can move around and access various chapters quickly and then put them together in the end.

You will have to play around with images, font sizes, colors and headers to make huge chunks of text easy to read. Make the book look attractive, easy on the eye and navigation friendly. In the end, put all the chapters together to create a seamless flow.

**Convert It into an eBook**

A simple Google search should give you multiple options for converting a word document into an eBook. You simply need to upload a Word file, and it is transformed into an eBook. A calibre is a free software that can be downloaded and used for word processor to eBook conversion. Go through everything to ensure the formatting is in place. If you are using Amazon Kindle Publishing (inarguably the best platform for eBook greenhorns), there's a preview tool that lets you see a final version of the book, so you know exactly how the formatting will appear on electronic devices.

## Create A Stunning Cover

You can create a gorgeous looking eBook cover using either some type of graphic software program such as Photoshop or Ms. Office (Powerpoint, Word, etc.). You can also hire the services of expert graphic designers on freelance project sites. Look at other covers for inspiration. Get a feel of them on the Kindle eBook store. Once you have a design and layout in mind, create and upload it. Amazon also has a handy cover creator, which can be used for building quick and effective eBook covers. Amazon will only display your book cover in the "Customers Who Bought This Item Also Bought" to trigger reader curiosity. Ensure that it is sharp, attention-grabbing and relevant.

## Pricing Your eBook

Amazon gives you the option of picking your own book pricing plan. You can either avail 35 percent profits by setting your own price or 70 percent profits by pricing your book according to Amazon's prescribed price between $2.99 to $9.99. Unless there is a strong business plan behind pricing your book outside $2.99 to$ 9.99, it makes sense to keep a significant chunk of your profits.

**Promote The Book Extensively**

Amazon will only boost your sale and reach when you fulfill the requirement of their sophisticated algorithms. You will have to promote and push your book initially to get support from them. This can be done by creating a few high-quality guest blog posts on sites/blogs related to your book. You can include a snippet about the book in the author bio to pique the interest of readers. Another great way is to take interesting and meaningful lines from your book and convert them into quote memes or tweets. Lots of people sharing and re-tweeting them will help you garner a large audience. Include a link to your book wherever permissible. Social media updates, blogs, email signatures and the likes.

A good way to build a bank of reviews and customers is to distribute free copies to people within your social network and ask them for genuine reviews. You can also price the book at a discounted rate in the early launch stages and ask the first few buyers to write reviews, before changing to the regular price. It always helps to have some reviews in there when readers are trying to make purchase related choices.

Another advantage of having a lot of early buyers is that Amazon boosts popular titles and gives it, even more, exposure once they see a lot of people picking it up. This can massively help your rankings.

## Other Publishing Channels

Other than Kindle Publishing, you can also publish your book on your own website. It may not enjoy a roaring exposure initially or at least not as much as a large platform like Amazon, however over a period of time; you can enjoy higher profits. Third party hosting merchants may charge you a small percentage fee of about 1 to 5 percent for accepting customer payments and delivering the content to them in a downloadable format.

# Chapter 2: Creating Killer Blogs

Blog- the internet marketer's golden word. And rightly so. Imagine creating a single valuable, detailed, comprehensive and well-researched post just once and earning from it years after you have published it. Blogs can be used in tandem with other passive income sources such as membership-based training programs or eBooks. They can also be stand-alone income generators. You can earn revenue through advertising programs such as Google Adsense. Then there's the highly lucrative world of affiliate marketing and list building. Selling banner advertisements, physical products, courses, eBooks and more is just the tip of the iceberg. There is really so much you can do with an informative, valuable and content-packed blog.

## Pack Value Which is Tough To Find Elsewhere

Pick a topic you are passionate about and know well. Do not incredible trend hop and know what topics are popular. Yes, you need to do basic keyword research to determine if there's sufficient demand for your niche but don't obsess too much about finding the most populated niches. The challenge is to grab any niche you like and make it popular! Go with specific topics or sub niches to laser target your audience and gain monopoly within the sub-niche. For instance, if you find that weight loss is an overcrowded niche, try dominating a sub-niche such as a post pregnancy weight loss or weight loss for seniors. This way you get a more focused audience who you can sell and market to with comparatively lesser competition.

## Create Interesting and Valuable Content

Create original, engaging, unique and useful content that gives your readers more value. Explore your expertise and write about something that you have a sound knowledge or background of. Use powerful elements to support your text such as images, videos, and infographics. Use screenshots wherever required to make the content clearer for your target audience. This will require more time and effort than a simple text blog. However, it will help your search engine rankings and will give you lots of loyal readers.

## Choose A Blogging Platform

If you are serious about starting a blog that generates passive income, avoid using a free blogging platform and opt for the WordPress self-hosted medium. WordPress is one of the most widely used, customizable, easy to operate and visually stunning blogging platforms. The self-hosted option allows you to set up banner advertisements and use affiliate market links within the blog. Your blog URL looks more professional, in addition to the fact that you will be able to play with abundant features for beautifying your blog. Find a reliable hosting service and a brandable, memorable and unique domain name.

**Blog Interface**

If content is the king, your blog design is the queen. It will determine many factors such as the stickiness of your blog, the time people spend on your blog, the click through rate of your links and much more. Opt for a clean, well-defined and user-friendly interface. Use can either use a WordPress theme or buy them from a third party like Themeforest.net. You can also pick between free and paid themes. Paid themes add more bells and whistles to your blog to make it look attention grabbing and professional. Themes can be changed instantly by going to the Appearances section of your WordPress admin panel. Ensure you pick a responsive theme for your blog as a majority of users access the Internet from handheld devices.

Make it easy for visitors to find everything on your blog by organizing all relevant tabs on your home page. Balance colors well, and leave enough white space to give the eye some relief. Use customized headers created by a professional graphic artist. Improve the readability of your blog by using subheads, bullets, text bubbles for critical text, tables, charts, illustrations and more. This helps attention starved people pick key points from your content without having to go through the entire piece.

## Monetizing The Blog

Advertising Program – You can 'rent' out space on your site to popular advertising programs such as Google Adsense, Yahoo Bing Network, Clicksor and more. These ad networks keep the advertisements relevant to your blog content and pay you a small amount every time a visitor on your site clicks on the advertisement. The best part is you aren't creating or selling any products but merely using the space on your blog to create passive income.

Affiliate Marketing – Affiliate marketing is all about selling other people's products on your site and earning a commission on every sale or lead that is fulfilled through a link on your blog. Say for instance, you run a pet travel site and have a steady stream of pet owners who travel with their pets. You can sign up as an affiliate for a puppy discipline informational eBook or a nationwide network of pet care and grooming services. So each time a pet owner buys the book or signs up for the pet grooming services, you get a nice little commission. Though individual products and services may have their own affiliate program, some popular marketplaces where you can find several affiliate programs are Clickbank, Offervault, Markethealth, ShareASale, Commission Junction and Avangate.

1. Review Writing – Writing useful, comprehensive and well-researched reviews is one of the best ways to sink your teeth into the world of affiliate marketing. Identify high-quality products with top-notch customer support, which can be really useful for your audience. Draft lengthy reviews to promote the products (include both pros and cons) and make your buyer's decision making process simpler. Reviews are often sought by people who are already half way within the buying cycle (with some options at hand) and giving them a good overview of the product will help you complete the sale.

2. Promote The Right Products – This should be fairly obvious yet it is surprising how many folks get it all wrong when it comes to promoting the right products. Find products that feature high ratings, superior quality, decent recommendations and most important – are relevant for your audience. Promoting dubious products and scams spell doom for affiliate marketers. You might make those first few sales by luring people, however your long term credibility may take a massive blow. If you plan to stick around for long and build a dependable source of passive income, pick your products judiciously.

3. Think Out Of The Box – If you believe the virtual world is already choc-a-bloc with multiple affiliate offers, think out of the box and act as an affiliate for local businesses. Use conventional businesses to generate profitable commissions. For example, let us assume you run an interior design and decorator blog that gives people interesting home makeover

ideas. You can tie up with home improvement companies, contractors and furniture suppliers in your neighborhood for lead capturing or selling their products to your readers. You may also be running a city or region based blog, and promoting local businesses may be the perfect passive income business model.

4. Diversify - Diversify your affiliate marketing offers, yet do not crowd your blog with too many sales pitches. Pick a handful of good offers and start promoting them. For example, for a travel blog, you can promote multiple products/programs such as backpacks, a traveler blogger training program, photography equipment and more. This way you are catering to diverse needs and pulling in bigger profits.

5. Links - Use link cloakers to get rid of the ugly, long and unprofessional looking affiliate links. They make your links appear cleaner, shorter and more

professional, while also boosting your click-through figures. Another pro tip is to make the visuals on your blog clickable. When images are made clickable by linking back to the sales page of the offer you are promoting, enthusiastic customers are immediately led to the relevant buying page. When you are eagerly looking to buy something or thinking about buying something, you don't want a tacky looking image upload page to play mood killer. User experience is a huge factor in determining the success of your affiliate marketing blog.

6. Selling Banner Ads – Once your blog attains considerable popularity, you can consider selling banner ad spaces to businesses related to your blog. You have complete control over how much you charge these firms since you are directly dealing with them. If you draw impressive traffic figures from a well-targeted audience, companies will be willing to negotiate lucrative advertising revenue.

7. Selling Informational Products – Selling your own digital products is another source of passive income. These can eBooks, short reports, email courses or membership programs. If you have high-quality, original and problem-solving content on your blogs, you will build a loyal base of readers who trust your expertise. They will be more than happy to buy informational products from you. The book can be sold to your mail subscribers or directly on your blog/website using an attention-grabbing landing page. You can also put the book for sale on the Amazon Kindle Publishing platform.

8. Directory Listings – When your blog becomes somewhat popular, you can start a paid listings section and rake in a good amount of income from it. The services can be related to your blog content. For instance, if you are running a blog related to wedding planning, and pull in a massive traffic of soon to be brides, you can put up listings of

professionals offering wedding related services such as florists, bakers, decorators, jewelers and travel companies. This helps to add an extra income avenue to your blog. Passive income is all about diversifying and optimizing revenue from a single source.

9. Pay Per Lead For Local Businesses – Imagine you have a thriving blog that focuses on real estate and attracts lots of real estate buyers and sellers who are hungry for information. How about working out an arrangement with local real estate firms/professionals to pay you per buyer/seller lead you send them? Leads can be captured by informing your audience that you can help them find some of the best properties in their area. It is a win-win situation for all. Again, passive income is thinking out of the box and leveraging multiple income streams to maximize your profits.

10. Promotions and Paid Recommendations/Reviews

– Once you gain considerable authority in your niche and are often referred to as an industry influencer, you can easily do paid reviews/recommendations or draft promotional posts. At this stage, you will most likely have a large following of people who trust your opinion. Cash in on it by promoting others' products and services through promotional posts. Make sure that you don't fill your blog solely with promotional posts and maintain a delicate balance between promotional and non-promotional content. The idea is not merely to sell to your target audience, but to help them buy by recommending really great stuff which makes their life simpler.

11. List Building – A blog that attracts a steady stream of targeted visitors can be great for list building. Place a sign-up box prominently on your blog to attract a swarm of organic subscribers from well-targeted traffic. These are a bunch of already interested action takers, and you could sell just

about any related offers, programs, courses, services and products to them. When people sign up for a mailing list, they are voluntarily expressing their interest in knowing more about the products/services being promoted by you. These leads can be used to generate a decent amount of passive income by boosting your sales conversions.

To get potential customers to sign up for your list, make them an offer they can't refuse. Throw in a free eBook or offer them a 10-15 day course. You can also include your affiliate links within the eBook or course. For example, if you are offering an eBook that offers WordPress site creation to beginners, you may want to suggest a good domain name registration and hosting service. Sign up as an affiliate of a reputed web hosting and domain name service and recommend it to your buyers in the course of the book.

# Chapter 3: Create Your Own YouTube Channel

Did you know that YouTube has 60 hours of video uploaded to it every 60 seconds? Or that more than 4 billion videos are watched every day? The platform gets a crazy 800 million unique visitors every month (source – Jeffbullas.com). There is a marked shift from consuming text related content to content that is more interactive and real time. Users with small attention spans find it way more convenient to see something than reading about it. Also, the demand for video-based content is at an all-time high, with lesser competition than text-based blogs. Not many people are confident about facing the camera, and that's where you can cash in while space is relatively less crowded.

## Belonging To The Big G Family Helps

Since YouTube comes from the Google stable, it is hugely favored by the big G in their organic search results. If you optimize your video for search engines by using the right keywords in the title, meta tags, and descriptions, your videos will enjoy higher placement rankings in search results. It is much easier to get a YouTube video to rank on Google compared to a blog post.

## Go With Technical and Problem Solving Topics

The nature of YouTube fits very well with technical and problem-solving topics where people are looking for very specific solutions. For instance, someone may want to know how to create a table of contents in MS Word or the basics of using MS Excel. Isn't it easier to get a step by step demonstration of using these features rather than only reading about them? Similarly, cooking, DIY crafts, and product demonstrations are extremely popular on YouTube.

When users watch videos on your YouTube channel, there are related ads that pop up on the screen. When visitors click on these ads, you get paid for it. This is why it is emphasized that you have a focused and clear problem-solving niche. Comedians or other YouTube performers may not enjoy much ad relevancy since they do not have a very targeted audience. However, if you are extremely popular, you may make a considerable income even with low click through rates.

Unconventional ways to approach a common topic works wonderfully on YouTube. Throw in a lot of wit, creativity, visual play and humor to illustrate complex topics. Offer interesting metaphors and analogies, and include surprise elements that make your audience take notice.

**Use Your Watermark For Videos**

Always use a watermark of your blog for your videos. This way users will know exactly where the videos originated from, which will make it easier for them to track your blog and channel. Some users may embed your video on their site. Having a clear watermark with your blog's name can drive more traffic and create a brand identity. Since descriptions only show up on YouTube and not other blogs where your video might be embedded, your URL can be made visible in the watermark.

**Start With An Overview**

Though videos are easier to watch than elaborate pieces of text, getting a user to watch an entire video is going be a challenge. How do you ensure that users are glued to your videos until the end? Simple. Just begin with an interesting overview of everything that's included in the video. This whets their appetite and keeps them hooked. This breaks the ice with your user, engages them and boosts their chances of sticking around. Get them interested and enthusiastic about what you are covering in your video. Make an interesting visual summary or map about what's coming up next. Giving them pointers about upcoming content is an excellent way to make them stay.

**Create A Fantastic Call To Action**

All your efforts of filming spectacular videos with the best sound and visual effects can be pointless if you do not include a compelling and impactful call to action at the end of it. Including a bright and attention-grabbing call to action ensures you don't leave your viewers high and dry after getting them interested with the video. They should know exactly what to do next if they want to know more about your products or services. Ask them to visit your website or blog or follow you on various social networks. If they sit through the entire video, they most likely are in a more positive and action oriented state of mind to follow what you tell them to do.

## Optimize Your Videos

One solid tip for optimizing your YouTube videos and making them more findable is to include your main keyword in the title followed by a subtitle that lists your secondary keyword and is a rephrased version of the main title. For instance, if you have a video talking about various retirement plans, you can title as Retirement Saving Plans: 30 Brilliant Tips For Planning a Hassle-Free Retirement.

Also, ensure your video descriptions are keyword optimized, appealing, clear and descriptive. This makes it easy for search engines to place them at the top of relevant searches.

**Leverage The Trailer Video Feature**

If you want to convert walk-in or browse through viewers into loyal subscribers, utilize You Tube's trailer video feature optimally. The platform allows you to include a video at the top of your channel to give nonsubscribers a glimpse of your channel. This acts as a teaser to pique your audience's curiosity.

Make a compelling, sticky and appealing trailer video to bag more subscribers.

Another super layout tip is to opt for the Player view over Grid View. Unlike Grid View, Player view sets a single large video on auto-play.

**Be Prolific And Upload Frequently**

There are no two ways about it. If you are looking to generate passive income from your YouTube channel, you must keep adding content prolifically. The more videos you have out there and the more consistently you post these videos, the higher are your chances of creating a decent income bank. Create an editorial planner and plan to post your videos at regular intervals.

Create and upload videos that talk about different

aspects of your niche/topic/industry to build an influential channel. For example, if you run a YouTube channel related to post-pregnancy weight loss fitness regimes, try and include other related information such as healthy recipes for new mothers or post pregnancy wardrobe ideas or newborn baby care tips. Try and explore the topic from varied angles, so visitors keep coming back for more.

# Chapter 4: Sell With Amazon FBA

Dropshipping is another convenient and lucrative online passive income option. A large number of virtual entrepreneurs prefer the drop shipping business model for its flexibility and simplicity. You don't need space to maintain a product inventory. Similarly, there is a minimal capital investment in setting up an e-commerce venture. While FBA (Fulfillment By Amazon) requires a flexible product investment, regular drop shipping doesn't need any upfront product investment.

The orders are fulfilled by a retail giant such as Amazon, while you get to make a tidy profit behind every sale. The best part about this business is that you can sell a huge variety of products without having to worry about maintaining a large inventory.

There's little wonder that FBA has become one of the most popular home business ventures.

FBA is a super way to leverage the power of Amazon for making profits. You do not have to deal with the sales, buyers or shipping process. Your only job is to source products and send them to Amazon for maintaining your inventory. Your products receive massive exposure in Amazon's marketplace. They store your product within their network of warehouses and deliver it to your customers. Heck, they even offer customer service. Couldn't be simpler, could it? An excellent way to rake in passive income, you say? Well yes and no. It is convenient and simple, but not a get rich overnight scheme. You need to invest considerable time and efforts in researching and identifying products that will sell like hot cakes. You will also need to find suppliers and negotiate prices with them. However, once you are all set, it can't get any more passive than this.

You literally don't have to do anything to bring in sales and deliver orders.

**Upfront Costs**

Unlike dropshipping, you will need a small investment to put together a product inventory for FBA and ship it to Amazon's warehouses. Other than physical product and forwarding charges, expenses you will incur include Amazon's referral fee, subscription fees (either 0.99/transaction or $39.99 monthly plan) and inventory storing fees.

The FBA calculator helps you work a selling price by considering exact fees and shipping charges. Your aim is to find unique products that people need at the right price and price them correctly to maximize your profits. The investment is completely up to the seller. You can buy products worth $10000 or $500. Start small to test your markets and scale up once you see results. Invest as much as you can afford to lose, pick your products carefully and price them judiciously.

If you are just getting your feet wet in FBA or sell more big ticket items in small quantities, you may be better off picking the $0.99/transaction subscription fee option. This plan lets you sell up to 40 products a month. However, if you reckon selling more than 40 products each month, it makes sense to sign up for the $39.99 monthly fee. This is good value for serious folks who plan to carry out hundreds of transactions each month. There are plenty of addition features, such as generating business reports in the latter.

**The FBA Edge**

What are the benefits of selling on FBA?

FBA items rank higher when people search for specific products. They also show up frequently on the recommended buy box option, even over items that are priced lower. Buyers are almost always likelier to opt for recommended products.

FBA products are eligible for Amazon Prime membership benefits like complimentary next day delivery, thus making Prime members much more likely to purchase these products.

You get access to a fantastic and widely used sales platform, enjoy higher search rankings, and a well-oiled, almost automated system that helps you generate huge profits consistently.

**Signing Up For FBA**

Start by heading to sellercentral.amazon.com. You

can either register for an FBA account with your existing credentials or create a brand new account. Pick your subscription plan depending on the number of products you expect to sell. You can either use your company's legal name or your name. Fill in your credit card number and other details. Credit card details are shared upfront so your account can be charged in the event that you run into a deficit. This can occur when you do not have any sales, yet have to bear warehouse storage and subscription fees.

Next, pick your display name. Remember, this is your brand identity. Make it unique, memorable and likable. Your audience must be able to identify and relate to it. It should be relevant to your niche if you are focusing on a specific group of products.

You will be required to confirm your identity with a phone call or text message. This completes your registration process. Fill in your bank account details so your earnings can be directly deposited into your account. The deposit method can be selected by going to the Setting tab and picking an option from the scroll down under Account Info. Verify your bank details to start receiving payments.

At this stage, you are an Amazon Seller but not yet registered for FBA. Now, visit the FBA registration page and hit on Getting Started to launch your FBA seller account.

**Finding the Right Products**

To begin with, you will have to be on the look-out for bargains and then measure them up against existing Amazon listings to anticipate how they will perform in comparison with competing products. How much can you sell the product for? Are the products likely to sell? Checking out existing products will answer these crucial questions. Use the Amazon Bestsellers list as a reference point to identify your star products. A product rank under rank 1000 in a relatively large category means it is faring reasonably well and can be considered for your inventory list.

Register to receive newsletter updates from reputed wholesalers or be a part of the mailing list of stores such Ikea and Walmart. They may send you special promos and offers or you can browse their website for popular or unique products. If you find a product that can be sourced really cheaply due to a limited period discount, try and order it in bulk and include it in your inventory. This way you can keep selling the product at a much higher price and rake in cool profits. Do not forget to take Amazon's fees into consideration while working out the price.

**Private Label Products**

Private label products are sold under your own brand name. You can source products in bulk directly from the manufacturer or wholesaler, and package the product with your label. You are therefore positioning the product as if it is being manufactured or supplied by your own firm.

## Chapter 5: Create Membership Sites

Membership sites can help you rake in a good amount of passive income for a long time if you have a particular expertise that is sought after by plenty of people, especially knowledge related to the virtual world. You may be an expert in creating smartphone apps or copywriting or web designing or basically anything that people actively seek to learn. It can also be related to DIY and hobby based pursuits. How about language learning if you have mastery over a particular language or drone making if you know how to put together incredible drones?

At the onset, it is important to understand that membership sites need hard-work. You always have to keep updating, adding value, provide novel information and much more to keep your paid subscribers hooked. You must offer beyond exceptional value to retain your subscribers, which means it may not be a good option if you are just starting out in the online business world. Once you gain sufficient experience in a domain, you can consider launching your own membership site based business model. If you possess unique skills or knowledge which is in-demand, you can jump into it after doing some basic groundwork. Since information is widely available everywhere, you must have something really unique to offer your audience if you expect them to pay for it.

**Adding Membership Option To Existing Blogs**

If your blog is already popular among a group of readers/users who are demanding more in-depth information from you, create a membership site and give them what they are looking for. For instance, if you run a blog that gives people ideas about what topics they can blog about or blog niche ideas and your audience suggest that you also include comprehensive keywords/keyword research reports for different niches, you can charge a premium membership fee for the detailed information. If you already have a blog or website, you simply need to add a membership site plug-in to it.

## Start With a Few Complimentary Slots

Start by giving out the first few slots for free to build some response and reviews for your membership based site. The most positive and active folks on your mailing list, who are always adding value in the form of suggestions or discussions, can be considered for the giveaway. You can also consider giving away the first few slots at a discounted price with a coupon mailed to your loyal subscribers.

You may have a set of people who are regularly commenting on your blog posts or social media, while also contributing meaningfully to the discussions and helping other members. Make them your evangelists. Make them feel privileged by offering them free membership, and let them spread the word about your membership site.

**Focus on Creating A Loyal Community**

Membership sites are as much about a supportive and loyal community feel as they are about power packed information. The information will pretty much fade away over a period of time. However, the relationship you build with your customers and the loyalty you inspire in them by adding value to their lives is what will keep them from leaving.

Membership sites are all about creating a dedicated community of users where people support each other, resolve each other's queries and offer valuable guidance. Build a passionate following on the social media, and create a learning forum where members can swap ideas and solve other's issues. Ensure that you are prompt in your response when subscribers mail you with an issue.

Always ask for feedback from active subscribers. What aspects of the topic do they want to know more about? What other tools and software they need to optimize their results? What are the most common issues they come across while doing what you teach them to? Opinion polls are a good way of identify the general sentiment related to various topics. You can build on topics that have been well-accepted and drop the ones that do not add much value.

You need to know exactly what your customers are

looking for to hand it to them on a platter. Unscreen is a handy tool for monitoring and analyzing your audience activity. It lets you know which content type is generating optimal traction so you can create more of those.

**Create High-Quality build**

Tutorials and guides are much sought after in today's information-packed digital world. People are looking for easier ways to perform multiple tasks. And what better to train people than to create high quality, interactive and information rich real time or pre-recorded videos. One of the biggest advantages of these videos is that they can be accessed by followers across the world according to their convenience. Ask questions, conduct polls and stimulate discussions to inspire greater user interactivity. This will keep your audience glued from start to finish.

Use high quality and evocative visuals to make the matter more interesting and digestible. Visuals can be creatively weaved into the narrative to explain tricky concepts. You need to have a rough draft of how your presentation will flow, even if you aim to keep it more spontaneous. Create a rough table of topics, which you can elaborate on during the course of the webinar. If you are catering to a more global audience, use more universally accepted words, gestures, and ideas.

**Organize Your Information Efficiently**

Once your site grows, you need to organize it effectively to foster better navigation and access to information for new members. Guide your members through the maze of information by putting it all together in an orderly manner. If you find that new or existing users are asking you the same questions over and over on the social media or email, you can put together a handy Q & A page for newbies.

Alternatively, have an introduction or 'begin here' page in place, where you can make new members feel less overwhelmed by all the information and guide them about navigating the available information in a step-by-step manner. Keep updating this section regularly.

Include a 'blast from the past' or 'refresher' section where you can re-post popular older blogs that members might have missed or link to those posts that are currently relevant.

**Record A Friendly Welcome Video**

One of the best ways to establish a warm rapport with your customers, and inspire their trust and loyalty is to record a cheery greeting video. It can be anything from a demonstration of how the site works or a story or a gentle reminder of the do's and don'ts. You can tell them how they can make optimal utilization of your services or how they can contact you should they stumble upon some issues or inspiring experiences of existing members.

**Bring In The Influencers**

You can offer free subscriptions to authoritative figures in your industry and ask them to leave behind genuine reviews about the site. People are likelier to take their unbiased report seriously, and give your site a look through. Since influencers have a relatively large follower base, your site will enjoy a wide reach among potential subscribers.

**Create Group Events**

Group events and challenges are a great way to engage existing members and keep them hooked. Motivate them and help them stay on track. It can be anything small like a challenge that helps subscribers attain a specific goal. For instance, if you run a membership site for writers who aspire to fulfill their writing goals, create a challenge video that encourages subscribers to complete a goal for the week. The buzz of working as a group/community can be wonderfully motivating and creates a strong, positive vibe. You can also have other events, team challenges (where members compete with each other), courses and similar activities frequently to keep your subscribers on their toes.

# Conclusion

Thank you for making it to the end of *Shopify: Create Your Very Own Profitable Online Business Empire! (Make Money from Home, Shopify, Dropshipping, Amazon FBA)*.  Hopefully, you have learned adequate information regarding how you can either start making money through Shopify, dropshipping, and Amazon FBA from scratch or how you can grow a business that you already have in existence.  Either way, there are many tools on the internet that can be easily accessed and can help you turn a good business into a great business from the perspective of profit.  If you follow through with the tactics that were presented in this book, there's no doubt that you'll be able to create greater streams of revenue for yourself.  These streams will then be able to provide you with the flexibility to make more money and find greater happiness for yourself.  It doesn't get much better than that.

Thanks again for reading this book!

# About The Author

Hi there it's Jonathan Walker here, I want to share a little bit about myself so that we can get to know each other on a deeper level. I grew up in California, USA, and have lived there for the better part of my life. Being exposed to many different people and opportunities when I was young, it made me want to strive to become an entrepreneur to escape the rat race path that most of my peers had taken. I knew I wanted to be able to travel and experience the world the way it was meant to be seen and I've done just that. I've travelled to most places around the world and I'm enjoying every minute of it for sure. In my free time I love to play tennis and believe it or not, compose songs. I wish you all the best again in your endeavours, and may your dreams, whatever they may be, come true abundantly in the near future.

www.ingramcontent.com/pod-product-compliance
Lightning Source LLC
LaVergne TN
LVHW012025060526
838201LV00061B/4460